I WILL survive

A PERSONAL STORY BY
Cerlisa Collins

I WILL Survive: Volume II- Limited Edition

Unless otherwise indicated, Bible quotations are from the Holy Bible, King James Version. All rights reserved.

The stories in this book reflect the author's recollection of events. Some names, locations, and identifying characteristics have been changed to protect the privacy of those depicted.

Manuscript editing
 Catherine LaCroix

Book Creation and Design
Ellese & Co Creative www.elleseandco.com

Publishing
Grace 4 Purpose Publishing Co.
Grace4purposeco.com
ISBN: 979-8-9926893-8-9

Printed in the United States of America

Foreword

Am I my sister's keeper? Yes, I am.

I remember the day my father told me that he and his girlfriend at the time were about to have a baby. I thought he had lost his mind. Nonetheless, the day I walked into that hospital and saw that face—the face that looked like my face, I was instantly in love.

Every step of her life I've been on the sidelines as Cerlisa has experienced traumas that no child should have had to. She had to fight to learn. She had to fight because of her looks. She had to fight with so-called friends and family. She had to fight for her life.

Nothing can prepare you for the call that comes at 4:00 AM to say that there has been an attempt on your sister's life. As I stood in that ICU looking over her comatose body with

my arms stretch to God praying for a miracle.
I knew that life for us all would be different.

Today, Cerlisa has laid bare her
experiences in hopes of helping someone
avoid the path she's had to walk.

I look in the eyes of this young woman who
has seen so much heartache and still stands
to fight another day. I see the soul of the baby
that I fell in love with, yet I know that within her
has been birthed a mighty warrior woman
with the WILL to SURVIVE.

Angela Cerel

biography

About Cerlisa

Cerlisa Collins is a force of nature. She is a 23-year old entrepreneur, a full-time student, and now an author. A series of traumatic events have caused Cerlisa to pause and share her experiences. The death of her parents, murder of her friend, and attempted murder on her life could have pushed her over the edge, but Cerlisa is DETERMINED to survive and thrive. She is the owner of CakedByCee, a mobile cupcake company, which focuses on providing old-fashioned, homemade sweet delicacies.

Cerlisa Collins, author

Check her business page out on
CakedByCee and **CakedBycee**

TABLE OF
contents

"When you are a kid, you don't realize you are also watching your parents grow up."

——————————— FACEBOOK MEME

Chapter 1

ONLY
one

My relationship with my parents was always complicated. Their relationship was complicated, so I often felt like I was in the middle of that. I was often at the center of their heated arguments, which made me feel very unsettled. While I loved my parents equally, I had a much better relationship with my father than with my mother.

My mom was very interesting. She was trained to go! She would cuss anybody out if she felt like they did her wrong, and she would not care. The problem was that she always felt attacked, so she was always in conflict with others. Sometimes, it would be embarrassing to be in public with her because you never knew what she would say. I don't know what made our relationship so bad. I never really understood why my mom and I bumped heads so much. Maybe it was because we were alike in so many ways. All I know is that most of the time, it was terrible.

I always felt like either she didn't want me to grow up, or she felt like she had to control me. I loved my mom. I just didn't understand some things she used to say and do to me. She screamed at me all the time. So, even as a child, I would yell back. Our relationship was built on this toxic foundation of fussing all the time. I remember always crying to my dad or calling my sister in tears. My sister was my escape. She would talk to me on the phone and often would end up taking a forty-five minute drive just to pick me up and get me out of the house.

Seeing my mom decline while I was going through my trauma was a different type of hurt. Her having stage 4 cancer was just a different kind of hurt, not knowing what would come next. We were on a mission to start treatment, but she declined too quickly. Everything went wrong, and because of that, she was too weak to receive any kind of treatment. I remember meeting with the cancer doctor one-on-one, where she sat me down, telling me everything that was happening and what was going to be the next steps. I cried so hard in the room with her. I was seeing my mom in her final days.

I became so numb to the situation that I could not shed any more tears. They would not come out. I was just so lost in what was going on around me. I wanted to know why the last two years of my life had to be like this.

I lost my dad, was shot and stabbed, and then lost my mom two and a half months later. I kept thinking, "make it make sense, please."

I remember the doctor called to come to say my goodbyes, and I was just all over the place. Walking in the hospital did something to me. It was so painful watching my mom as she suffered through the pain, moaning and groaning while nothing could help her at this point.

I gave her a kiss, made peace, prayed, told her I loved her, and I left the room. Four days later, I was lying in bed when I got a call. I knew what the call was, and I just broke down. I couldn't really say anything. I made my way down the highway back to Richmond, and the whole way back, I worshiped God in my car and cried. I then realized I couldn't call my mom or dad anymore...

Fortunately, I was able to make peace with my mom before she passed, but it will take many more years of therapy before I can ever understand why things were as bad as they were.

My relationship with my father was the polar opposite. I was, and forever will be, a daddy's girl. My dad was the one who taught me about life. He was the one I would talk to when things got tough. He was the one who taught me how to manage my money. He was the one who taught me "If at first you don't succeed, try and try again" My daddy would always talk with me about how to carry myself as a woman, everything I do in life, and respect myself. He would also talk to me about financial things, teaching me about managing money and credit scores at an early age. No matter how much my parents fought, he was always there for me, to lift me and support me. I received a lot of good advice from my dad, and I wouldn't be the smart woman I am today if it wasn't for him.

I remember one time when I came home crying to my dad because I was getting bullied at school. The next thing I knew, it was time for me to go to school the next day. My daddy walked me to the bus stop with his pistol on his hip. As I reflect on it, I'm not exactly sure what he would do with it.

But he always made me feel safe. My daddy did not play about me. He always made me feel like I was important and that he loved me. He was always supportive and helped me learn things I needed to know to grow up.

My daddy was also a comedian. He had an awesome, funny personality. He was the life of the party, the light bulb in a lamp, the glue that literally held every day together. He was always laughing and joking. To know my daddy was to love him. I miss him so much. I just wish I could sit on his lap, cry, and tell him how life has been going for me. He was the one to pick me back up when I was done. It's like he could fix everything wrong. He didn't always tell me what I wanted to hear, but he told me the truth, whether I liked it or not.

Losing my father was one of the worst experiences of my life—when my dad passed away, and my sister finally told me he was dead. In the weeks leading up to his death, he had left Virginia to visit some friends and family in Kentucky. While traveling, an aneurism burst, and he never made it back to Virginia alive. It was so hard for me to believe. I remember calling my older brother, Cerron because he was at the hospital where my father was. I FaceTimed with him so that I could see my dad—and that sealed it for me. I couldn't believe I was looking at my dead father. I couldn't believe I was twenty-one years old and planning my daddy's funeral. I didn't know how I was going to move on with my life without him. I didn't know how to grieve at the time. That was a major loss for me. I picked up so many bad habits after that moment. And in some ways, I became more vulnerable to the likes of the man who tried to kill me two times because I was trying to fill such a big void in my life.

I wasn't the only one that was heartbroken. Mama was so heartbroken when she found out my dad had passed away. It hurt me to see her so hurt. My mom continued hurting because of my dad's passing until she eventually died. I feel like because he was no longer here with her that she made herself sick. I really believe that heartbreak kills. I was so stressed out dealing with my mom because she didn't know how to deal with my dad's passing. She cried every day. Every time I would come around, she would cry.

Whenever I came to visit, she tried to cling to me. It came to such a point that I had to set boundaries. I couldn't let myself go and hover around my mom constantly. When all was said and done, I never imagined I would be twenty-three, having lost both of my parents and trying to figure out how to navigate my life.

"Everyone you meet is fighting a battle you know nothing abo kind. Always."

————————————ROBIN WILLIAMS

Chapter *2*

SCHOOLIN'
life

As I reflect on it, my strong resolve to fight was really fortified as early as age six or seven. It was then that I felt I had to learn to protect myself. Elementary school was the worst for me. I had a hard time dealing with the bullies — and let me tell you, I had to deal with quite a few of them. The girls in school would tease me, call me names, and it was so hurtful. I was quiet and kept to myself most of the time, but they would still seek me out, calling me "Barbie" and pulling my hair. Ironically, nearly all the teasing started with my hair. In retrospect, I believe it was because I naturally had the type of hair that their parents had to buy for them. And now that I am an adult, I know that it was jealousy. That didn't make it any less painful or scary as a child, though. I tried to avoid walking down certain hallways because I didn't want to run into them. I knew they would make fun of me and do stupid stuff.

I think I was about ten years old when I was diagnosed with alopecia. I started to have terrible hair loss and bald patches on my head. It was so painful knowing that I would have to get injections in my scalp for the rest of my days. I had to get treated constantly for a couple of years, and then it started to lighten up. Now it comes and goes. Sometimes, I'll go through a period when I'll start getting a lot of spots, and sometimes it's nothing. The irony of it all was that the very thing that kids teased me about was the thing that I struggled with.

The first trip to the dermatologist was the most traumatizing for me. The doctor pulled out this huge needle that she had to use for multiple places in my scalp! It was the absolute worst. Eventually, I got used to it. Until this day, I still see the dermatologist for alopecia. But I can say now that I have so much hair that you'd never know about the hair loss!

I had this physical education teacher in high school who always checked on me, ensuring I was okay. She knew about the bullies and knew I was always upset behind them. She always tried to talk with me positively, telling me that everything would be okay. She was the absolute best. I would sit in her classroom during lunch or between classes.

It became so awful that whenever people would touch me, I would just snap. One time,

I was in high school and it was a tornado drill. A boy touched my butt while we were in the middle of the drill, and I completely lost it. I beat him over the head with my history book. And I was the one who ended up in trouble. For me, school was not a safe place. One girl in high school, in particular, was the worst. She picked on me constantly. One day, she followed me into the bathroom and pushed me into the trashcan. I felt so humiliated. I always used to cry because I couldn't understand why people would treat me this way. I've always had problems with girls. I was the stereotypical light-skin, pretty girl with long hair—and they hated me because of it. The constant bullying since grade school made me not trust people, and it made me really standoffish with girls.

As I was going through these issues, I began to develop a relationship with my neighbor. He was a couple of years older than me. We would hang out occasionally. After high school, I was so desperate to move out of the house that he and I got an apartment and started building a life together. But we were both young, and I don't think either of us understood the responsibilities of having an adult relationship. Yet, even after we went our separate ways, he remained someone I could turn to for help or call. When we broke up, I moved into a townhouse, and this was my first time really living on my own. I was still young but moving back to my parents' house was not an option. I was determined to have my own home and live an independent life.

"When people show you who they are, believe them."

——————————————— MAYA ANGELOU

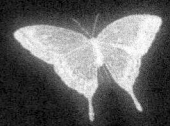

Chapter 3

DEVIL'S
dance

There is ongoing litigation regarding my relationship with this individual, so I don't want to use his real name. For the purpose of this book, we will just call him Satan.

When I first met Satan, I thought he was the best thing ever. I thought he gave me what I was looking for and what I was missing from a relationship. He spoiled me. It wasn't that he was materialistic, but he liked nice things—and he liked for me to have nice things. That was how he showed his love. On the weekends he was off, he would always take me somewhere, and we would go out of town to D.C., to a really nice restaurant just to hang out and spend time together.

At the beginning of our relationship, he treated me like a queen. He would give me a heads up when he came home, so I didn't have to cook when he brought us dinner. In the mornings, he would leave money for me to get my nails and my feet done.

He would randomly send me money for lunch, get my hair done, or pay a bill. I thought that the feelings he showed me and how he would try to take care of me was him being protective. It was not. As I think back on it, I never really learned to tell the difference between when someone wants to protect you and when someone wants to possess you.

I started to realize that things were wrong and weren't what they seemed to be around November or December 2019. Then, I found out I was pregnant in December 2020. I remember calling my best friend, crying tears of joy. I kept thinking, "oh wow! I'm about to be a mom." I was so happy but nervous at the same time. But that came to an end shortly after I found out. Just before the New Year, I had a miscarriage. I think Satan was more devastated than I was. He cried like a baby when it happened, the rest of the day and the following days. Then, from that point on, he started to treat me badly and started to act weird.

I remember UPS dropped shoes off at our door one time, but they had delivered them to the wrong house. We took the shoes inside, not knowing who they belonged to. After a while, we got a note on the door asking if we had received a box. I pulled the note off the door and brought it inside. I called Satan to let him know that he had to call these people and see if they would come to get their box when he got home. It turns out that they were very impatient and wanted to know if we had the box right away. Back then, I was still pregnant and not feeling well. When they came banging on the door and peeping through the window, I called Satan, and he came racing back home.

He took his gun and went outside. I was getting more nervous at this point. I could hear him screaming and hollering at these people outside. I couldn't make out everything he was saying, but I knew that he was upset they were peeking through the window while I was home alone. It turns out that Satan pulled the gun out on these people and their little girl! I couldn't believe it.

Next thing you know, about seven police cars were swarming the apartment. I get that he was mad and trying to be protective, but I started to notice that he let his anger get the best of him and took things way too far.

We started to argue a lot over the craziest, most petty things ever. He would get so mad. One time, he got mad at me because I didn't want to have sex right then and there, so he started an argument. I decided to go out for a ride to clear my head instead. I left the house and rode around downtown, which I would often do when I wanted to think about things. I love the Richmond landscape, and riding around downtown would help me think.

When I returned to the apartment and put the key in the door to go inside, he had locked me out of the house! Not only had he locked the house, but he had also pulled the couch against the doorknob of the front door so that I couldn't turn the knob. I stood outside and knocked for what felt like thirty minutes before he finally let me in. I guess because I was so loud, he eventually let me in the house, but it was a whole big fuss just for me to get inside. The smallest things turned into something big every single time.

We went out of town one time, and of course, he got in his feelings about something stupid and started to fuss with me, so he walked back into the hotel to get something, and I stayed in the car waiting for him to get back. I opened my phone and started scrolling Facebook. I clicked on this video that was on my timeline. So he tried to "catch me doing something." He walked up to the back window on the driver's side. He then opened the door and said: "So you gone FaceTime a nigga while you with me. You out here on FaceTime with another nigga." He just kept screaming and yelling. He then took my stuff in the car, threw everything in the street, and spit in my face. I was speechless and so embarrassed. I picked up my things from the ground, crying because I just didn't understand why he was like this.

Why did he always assume crazy things? How did watching a video turn into me talking on FaceTime with a dude?

That incident should have been all the warning I needed, but I was all over the place emotionally back then, and I wasn't paying attention to the signs. The next big argument happened on Christmas. We argued because I didn't get him the pair of shoes that he wanted. He didn't like the shoes I picked out for him, so he started arguing with me, calling me names like bitch and whore. He then began throwing things all around the house. He was having a full-on meltdown over some shoes. I was so afraid. I honestly couldn't believe it. I knew at that time that I needed to leave him, but I wasn't sure how to do it.

At the time, he still had his apartment, and I still had my townhouse. We were planning to move into my townhouse once his lease was up in the spring, but I was beginning to think that it wouldn't be such a good idea anymore.

I remember one time we were on our way to dinner for a date. I was giving him attitude about something, refusing to talk, and he could not take it. He started saying trifling things and threatening to turn the car around and go back home. I was like, "Okay, cool. Whatever. I don't give two shits." He then opened a water bottle and poured the whole bottle on me before hitting me in the head with it. I literally couldn't do anything but cry. He just so evil and mean. What did I do to make him pour water on me? It leaves you with a stuck face like dude you really just poured a bottle of water on me? He continued to drive towards the restaurant and then started to be apologetic, saying "I'm so sorry" "I'll give you money to get your hair done" "I know I should've just respected you not wanting to talk".

There was one incident where we were arguing, and he got mad to the point where he gathered all of my belongings at his house and started throwing my things around the house. He then threw all of my belongings outside, even on the front lawn. I cried and called my mom and best friend to come help me get my things and take them to my place. I was so embarrassed. The neighbors came outside to ask if I was okay and if I needed help with anything. Eventually, we squashed the tension, and I went back inside, but things continued to go downhill.

Things came to a head in July 2020. It was the first time he tried to kill me. We had gone to D.C. for his birthday. Things had gone well for the most part. I mean, our relationship was strained, but I still loved him and thought we might be able to work things out. We were in the hotel room, and we stepped outside of the room so I could take a picture of him. I had his phone in my hand, and I was taking a picture of him when this girl popped up on his screen. I just looked at him and kind of smirked at him. He knew that he was in hot water then. He snatched the phone from me and started screaming at the top of his lungs. We stepped back into the hotel room, having a very heated argument. He picked up a chair and threw it at me.

At that moment, I was so angry. I remember thinking to myself: "You know what, I'm not doing this shit tonight. I want to go back to Richmond." I started packing my bags, and he began packing his as well. We walked downstairs to get in the car, and before I could even get my bags in the car, he pulled off and left without me.

There I was, stranded in D.C. with no way to get back home. I started calling friends in hopes that someone would be able to help me. I called my friend Stylo because I knew he had a cousin who lived in Woodbridge. Just about that time, Satan came back around to the hotel and forced me into the car. We started to pull away when my phone vibrated, and he snatched it out of my hand. He read the text message where I asked my male friend to get me, and he became so unhinged. Like I had never imagined. He started screaming obscenities at me. He accused me of having sex with the guy because I had asked him to help me get out of D.C. In retrospect, it felt like he was just looking for a reason to justify beating me. And he did. For hours. Driving down Interstate 95.

We hadn't even left the hotel parking lot when he started punching me over and over in the car. He would pull my hair. He kept hitting me in the eye and nose. I tried to fight back, but I was trapped in the car. I kept trying to roll down the window to scream for help, but he locked it. I got so disoriented because he was driving aimlessly around the city, screaming at me, and hitting me. I was so afraid, and I didn't know what was going to happen. I tried to open the door to the car, but he wouldn't let me. As we were still riding around the city, he started to take my belongings and threw them on the side of the road. All my clothes were now gone. My purse, my laptop, everything that I had with me, he threw them out of the window. He even threw my dad's ring out of the window. I watched helplessly as he threw away so many important things to me as if they were trash. What was important to me meant nothing. After about an hour or so of riding around the city, he eventually got onto the highway. We rode down the highway, then he got off at the exit and came back around to show me all of my stuff.

As the night went on, it got even more bizarre and frightening. He got off at the exit and came back around to pick up my purse. I remember thinking, "You've done all of this, but you decide to go back and get my purse?" He left everything else lying there on the side of the road, including some memorabilia from my father's passing that I will never be able to get back.

The next three hours were torture like I never imagined experiencing. He would calm down a little bit before having these mood swings full of rage. When he did that, he would get more and more reckless each time. I remember him accelerating until he hit ninety or a hundred miles per hour, and then he would slam on the brakes. It felt as if he was doing that just to make me hit my head. After five minutes or so, just when I thought he was beginning to calm down, his rage would well up again, and he would turn and spit in my face. It was so humiliating. At one point he stopped the car, got in the backseat with me and just broke down saying "Cerlisa please I'm sorry, I'm sorry for all of this. I'm sorry for hitting you, just please forgive me". I'm crying wishing he would just take me home, I wouldn't say anything back in fear he would hit me again then BOOM! He punches me in the face and gets back in the front seat and pulls off.

At the time, I still had my phone. I called my mother, my sister, and his mother. All of them tried to talk to him so that we could get home safely, but nothing was clicking. Fortunately, I was able to share my location with my sister, and she was able to contact the state troopers. I wanted to share my location with my sister so she could contact the state police, and they would be able to track my phone to see where I was. But as he continued to display what I believed to be very erratic behavior, he snatched my phone and threw it out of the window. There I was with nowhere to run. No one on the other end of my phone. Frightened and alone.

We had made it down as far as Stafford County when he pulled off at the exit and started screaming at me—once again in a rage. He dragged me out of the car to the side of a shopping center. The only thing I remembered seeing was a Taco Bell and a Tropical Smoothie. He pushed me into a wooded area and knocked me to the ground as he was beating me. I fought him off as best I could and was able to crawl to the edge of the woods. Like an animal striking his prey, he jumped onto my back and started strangling me. This would be the first time I had to fight the devil for my life.

He put all of his strength into strangling me. In my opinion, it was only by the grace of God that I was able to turn over and get him off of my back, so he could stop closing my airway. After that, he told me to get back in the car. I had no idea what was going to happen, but I got back in the car. I was so tired from fighting, and I knew that my best chance of surviving was that he would just get tired of beating me.

He must have gotten tired because we were able to make it back to Richmond without another incident. He drove back to the neighborhood where I lived and dropped me out of the car in the middle of the road. I walked back to my house. I immediately changed my clothes because he'd ripped them off of me. We had left D.C. before midnight, and it was almost five in the morning by the time he finished torturing me.

My first instinct was to drive to his mom's house. She lived the closest, and I needed to use the phone to let everyone know I was okay. While I wanted to go to her house to make those calls, I think it was more than that.

I had for months found comfort in his mom. She was nice to me, and she was also very maternal. She understood the challenges I had with him, and she was able to help me deal with the abuse. She, herself, had been abused by Satan's father, so she understood how complicated those emotions were for me.

I mustered the strength to drive to his mom's house, and I rang the doorbell. I just remembered this traumatized look on her face when she saw me. She was fully aware of all that had transpired because she had been on the phone pleading with him to bring me home and let me go. But the look on her face when she saw me was as if she had seen a ghost. Well, maybe the look on her face as if she had seen her ghost. I felt when she looked at me that she saw the reflection of everything she had been going through relived in her son. And she looked shocked.

So, I used her phone to call my mom and sister. My sister told me to stay there and that she was sending her husband to come to get me to take me to the hospital, so I could get checked out and make sure that my face was okay and I didn't have any broken bones. Little did I know, my brother-in-law was already in Richmond because he had driven into the city from where they lived to see if there was any activity at my house.

Before I even left the house, his mom started begging me not to tell the police. And honestly, I really didn't want to get the police involved. The whole situation was so embarrassing. Also, a piece of me felt like he didn't mean to do all the things that he had done. I mean, who does these things to someone they love? How could I have allowed myself to care so deeply for someone that could do this to me? And why the hell is his mama trying to talk to me about not pressing charges when her son just tortured me for five hours and tried to strangle me?

I should have known then that for as much as I loved her—and sometimes even felt like I needed her because she was the only one who could understand—she had no loyalty to me.

What I now know is that this is how abuse and codependency work. This incident set off months of calls from his family to drop charges and pressure from my family for me to never see him again and not to have anything to do with him. And I still wanted answers. I wasn't able to just stop seeing him. It took a while. He always threatened me that if I left him or started seeing anyone else, he would harm me, that I would come up missing, or he would simply kill me. It took me finding a connection with people in my life who genuinely loved and supported me for me to be able to set the boundaries that I needed with Satan. And, while it did take me a few months, I eventually stopped feeling something for him. I was moving on with my life. I could never have imagined that I would have experienced an even worse, more heinous horror at his hands.

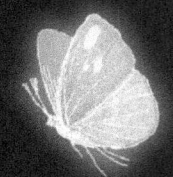

"Number one question I'm asked, other than about me being a twin, is 'why are you so caring?' It's because I want everyone to feel loved even if they don't treat me right. It's mandatory for me."

— WILLIAM SIMPSON
MARCH 5 , 2019

Chapter 4

WILL
power

When William came into my life, I learned the difference between what it means when a man tries to possess you and when he tries to protect you. William saved my life, and I am here to tell the story because of him.

When I first met William, we were just chilling, hanging out with friends. We connected instantly. In addition to being a very attractive man, he was very soulful. Our early conversations were always about deep topics. I trusted him enough to tell him about my abusive relationships. From the very beginning, his true character shone through. He just couldn't understand how any man would abuse a woman. He told me that I would never have to worry about him hitting me. I felt safe with him. I showed him a picture of what my face looked like in the hospital after Satan beat me up, and he got tearful.

I not only felt safe with William, but he was so very empowering. William was so chill, calm, relaxing, and funny. He always poured love and light into me. He wasn't overprotective and always protected me when he needed to, but if anything, he was going to pour love and light into me and wisdom and encouragement. He would text me good morning every day or say something encouraging to start my day. He could always tell when I was having a bad day. He would say something positive or just see me to make me feel better. Being very supportive, knowing what I was going through at the time. He always reminded me how beautiful and strong I was and that no man should ever put their hands on me no matter what the situation is.

We became fast friends, and I always felt like he motivated me to be the best person I could be. William was a very hard worker. He and his twin brother own a detailing business "The Twinz Mobile Detailing". They would come to you to wash your car, detail your car, and do a lot of other things including yard work. He was also deeply rooted in his faith. He would work with his church as well. I know on Sundays him and his brother would help record the church service. He would leave his full-time job to go to his part-time job in the detailing business. He was goal-oriented and always appeared to have his head in the game. His drive inspired me. His faith inspired me. His loving spirit protected me.

We grew closer each passing day. We spent Christmas and Thanksgiving together. He came to chill with my family and me on both holidays and came to my mom's on Christmas, where we laughed and had fun. He loved my mom's mac and cheese. I remember one time my mom made a great big pan just for him. My mama loved some William. Almost every time that we talked on the phone together, she'd say: "What's William doing? You talked to William today? How are the twins? Are they working hard today?" He'd come to visit me and end up doing some work around the house or be outside picking weeds out my flower garden. I remember one time, he said that he was on the way, and I looked at my ring doorbell because it said there was motion at the front door, so I looked through my phone, and he was outside washing my car. He was the sweetest.

He was also the best landscaping person on this earth. Back in March, he redid my flower garden in my front yard, and let me tell you, that boy did the damn thing. It looked amazing! I recall one day William and I were having a conversation about just any and everything, and he said: "You know Cee, we might not be together.

God may have just placed me in your life to show you that there are good men out here, to show you that you don't have to be abused mentally, physically, or emotionally. You don't have to be hit on and called names. There are genuine men out there that will give you the world." And now that I think back on that conversation, I can't help thinking, "Wow, if that was the case, why did it have to happen this way?"

On May 2, 2021, William and I came home from a night out with our friends. He came back to my house as he would often do. While he and I were not dating, we had grown very close and were physically intimate. On this particular night, we had gotten in the shower together. As we were showering and getting ready for bed, we heard a big noise. I looked at William and said, "What was that?" But he replied that he didn't know. As I pulled the shower curtain back, Satan burst through the bathroom door and opened fire on us at close range. He shot me four times, but the only shot I felt was in my knee. It felt like he had lit a match and set me on fire. It felt like I was burning up. I was screaming, crying, and begging him to please stop. William grabbed me to protect me and told Satan to stop, but he kept firing.

As William laid in the bathtub bleeding to death, Satan grabbed me from William's arms and began pistol-whipping me. Then Satan grabbed me by my left arm and dragged me out of the bathroom, down the steps. In the kitchen, he proceeded to grab a knife and stabbed me. He stabbed me in my neck, the back of my head, and on the side of my vagina. As he was stabbing me, I heard the ambulance. I begged him just to leave because the police were coming. Something jolted him, and he ran out of the house.

I don't know where I got the strength to get help, other than sheer will and determination. I heard the voice of my father telling me to get up off the floor. I knew that I didn't want my mother and my sister to find me this way.

So, I got up.

Somehow, I was able to crawl to the front door to get help. I was naked, drenched in blood from head to toe, in shock. But I was determined that I would tell the police who did this to me—who did this to my friend. I don't remember much after the police arrived, but I do remember lying in the back of the ambulance and receiving a jolt of electricity racing through my body as they shocked me back to life. I remember being in the hospital and being constantly drugged with all these medicines and receiving shots in my stomach. I remember the pain. I was in so much pain. My mom would come to the hospital every day during visting hours from 8am–8pm to spend time, keep me company and bath me. My mom was so hurt seeing me laid in a hospital bed in a cast, legs wrapped from bullet wounds and a tube hanging from my neck. Every so often she would just cry and say, "I can't believe he did my baby like this". Indeed my mom was suffering like I was. Visiting hours would come to a end and my mom would be packing to head home, it was the most depressing thing to see. I didn't want my mom to leave. I sobbed every night because I didn't want to be alone, I was terrified to be in ICU.

The physical pain paled in comparison to the emotional pain and trauma I felt. I was so vulnerable. Here I was, twenty-three years old, and my friend had lost his life at the hands of my ex-boyfriend. I was so afraid his family would hate me. I already felt such guilt, and the thought that people would blame me for this was soul-destroying. But it was the exact opposite.

One of the most affirming and healing conversations was a conversation I had with William's mother. I didn't know her well, as my relationship with William was relatively new. But in three or four sentences, she showed me what the love of Christ looks like in a person. She said: "I'm not ready to talk right now, and one day I will be. But you need to know this is not your fault." What was so healing for me was that she didn't pretend not to be devastated. She didn't even pretend that it would be easy to see me or to look at me. Yet, she still represented the love of God. It was as if she could see my brokenness and guilt and said no—I'm not going to let you blame yourself for this. The whole family represented the love of God for me. They have called or sent me text messages to check up on me. I have stayed in contact with his brother from the moment when I could communicate once I left the hospital.

At the end of the day, not only did William save my life, but his loving spirit gave me the will to keep living, and to tell my story so that other women won't have to experience what I did.

[1] Whoever dwells in the shelter of the Most High will rest in the shadow of the Almighty.[a]

[2] I will say of the LORD, "He is my refuge and my fortress, my God, in whom I trust."

[3] Surely he will save you from the fowler's snare and from the deadly pestilence.

[4] He will cover you with his feathers, and under his wings you will find refuge;
his faithfulness will be your shield and rampart.

———————————————————— PSALM 91

Chapter 5

WHAT'S
next

So here we are four months later, and the story is still unfolding. May 2nd started what seems like an endless series of surgeries and court appearances. Life is just different and weird, but at the same time, I'm beyond blessed. I've come so far since May 2nd. Life is definitely different. In this season, I've learned so much about myself and the people around me. Sometimes, it takes tragedies like this to see who a person really is, who is here for you, and who is not. It has shown me who to give my time and energy to and who doesn't deserve it. It has also taught me to focus on the type of person I want to be and connect with my true self.

It is a truly powerful moment in self-growth when you can sit back and acknowledge that the people around you haven't changed but that you have changed. I see my life more clearly now. It's times when I try to make out how I'm still moving, how I still have the strength to keep going. It's times when I just want to give up and say forget it all, but I've come way too far to give up now, and I have the power to be great and overcome everything that has happened to me. I know my mom and dad would want me to keep going.

It's days when I struggle to go to sleep at night. I find myself getting sad and depressed when the sun starts to go down and the night falls in. I start to tear up. I try to be strong and stay busy, so I don't cry, but it's hard, very hard to do. Sometimes, I just start praying. I ask God to bring me out of this darkness. Help me in this season, God. Show me that I have a purpose and that I am loved. Help me become who I want to be, help me shine my light.

There was a time when I wished I would've stayed lying on my kitchen floor and died. I felt like I wouldn't have to suffer and face all of what was going on. But again, I didn't want my mom and sister to walk into the house and see me lying dead on my kitchen floor. Waking up in the morning is the same. I struggle to get out of bed. Those are the days when I want to lie there and cry a river, from missing my parents and hurting over what has happened to me. It's just tough. The last few weeks, I've been a wreck while waiting for the trial and surgery. I wish I could just call my parents and talk with them.

Aside from the difficult days, life is still good. Every day isn't a good day, but it's still beautiful. Before the incident where Satan tried to take my life, I started a cupcake business, and it is still growing. And my business is flourishing. The love shown is amazing. I have customers inquiring from out of state about my cupcakes.

I'm truly blessed. And I do all that I can to keep things moving. I got my notary license in the midst of all this madness. I'm enrolled at Old Dominion University, this is my last year, and I moved to a new place.

Most importantly, I'm sharing my story. At times, it feels overwhelming to put in words all that has happened, but I've felt it is very important for me to do so. You see, there is a twenty-three years old woman out there who is involved in an abusive relationship, and she is too afraid to leave. She's too embarrassed to tell her family what is really going on. She's too ashamed. She's too conflicted about her feelings because she sees good in him, even though he does bad things to her. I needed to write this story to tell that woman: "Fuck that man! He means you no good. You are strong enough to choose you, even if you can't see it right now."

Back in March, I was picking my classes for the next semester, and I chose a class called Gender-Based Violence, not knowing I was a serious victim of domestic violence. Taking this class has opened my eyes to what was going on with me. It showed me the red flags I was ignoring. I had to watch a video for a homework assignment, and it's like I was reliving the relationship all over again. The man would hit the woman and then five minutes later said: "I'm sorry, I love you and I won't do it again. Just please forgive me, and I'll make it up." All those things happened to me, and I believed it wouldn't happen again.

It's the little things that help me get through my day-to-day life, especially going to church on Sundays. I try to go to church every single Sunday if I'm not out of town. Church just fills me up. It gives me hope, confidence, and comfort that I will have a great week. The pastor at Cedar Street in Richmond, VA could not possibly know just how many times I've felt like his messages were tailored just to me.

My second surgery was successful. I was anxious and scared because if you know me, you know I was in excruciating pain with the first surgery. It was the absolute worst. The nerve block and pain medicine didn't work. I was hurting for almost two months. But with this surgery, I've been able to tolerate the slight aches and pain.

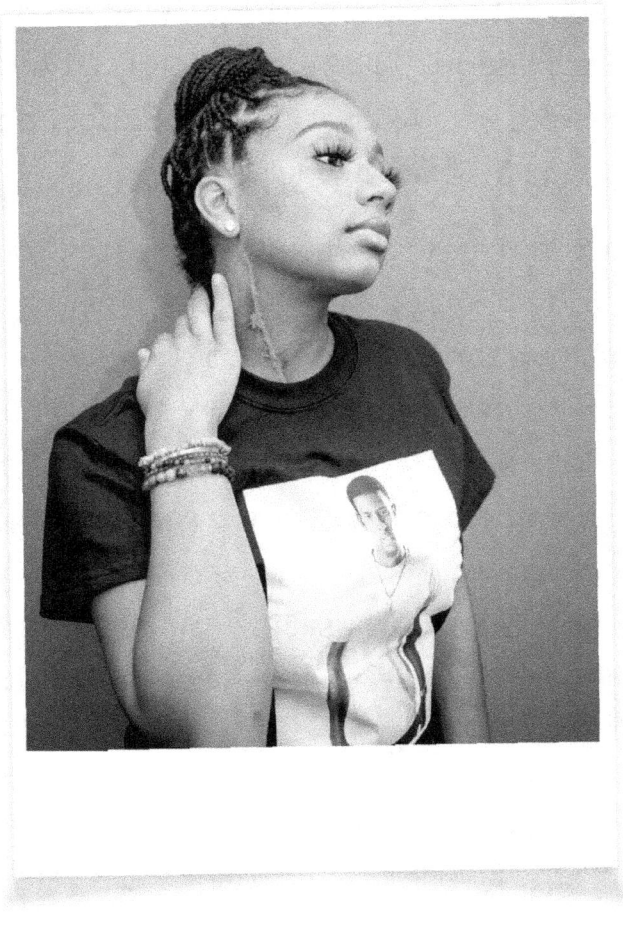

With everything going on, I get caught up in my head, fighting with myself, and going to church makes it easier for me at times. I got a lot of devotionals, morning prayers, evening prayers, and encouragement books when I first got out of the hospital, so every morning, I wake up and read my morning prayer and encouragement. I read a passage out of my devotional book and do the same thing at night before going to bed. I've been trying to stay committed, even though things are tough. I'm not here because I earned it, I'm not here because I deserved it, I'm here because Jesus kept me in MIND!

People often ask me how I do it. All I can say is, through God's grace, I have the WILL to survive.

Chapter 6

WOUNDS INTO
wisdom

People think healing is some pretty little process wrapped in candles and prayer. But healing after trauma? It's messy. It's loud. It's lonely. And most of all, it's REAL WORK.

After I survived being shot, stabbed, and left for dead, I didn't just wake up one day and feel whole again. I had to fight for my healing the same way I fought for my life. And just like surviving, healing came with its own kind of pain.

In the early days, I tried anything I could to calm my mind. I called it, "Chinese Heaven"-vibrational frequencies I'd listen to while on my mama's couch, my arm in a cast, my spirit shattered. The pain in my body was bad, but the ache in my soul was worse. My mama-who was hurting too, hiding cancer we didn't know about yet-was packing my bullet wounds at night, while we both tried to survive our own hinds of pain. That house was full of love, but also full of struggle. Sometimes, pain makes it hard to show up the way you want to for the people you love.

Eventually, I had to move out. I needed peace. I needed air. So I moved in with my sister, Angela, and her boys. It was loud, chaotic, and humbling. Sharing a bathroom with teenage boys? Whew. But it forced me to grow. It forced me to give up that, "everything to myself" mindset. For the first time, I was learning how to exist in a house gull of people. Even though it stretched me, it healed me too.

Physical therapy was a whole other battle. The first time they took off my cast, I cried. My arm was discolored and deformed, and I didn't know if I'd ever feel normal again. But I had a physical therapist who didn't play about my recovery. She didn't flinch at my tears. She pushed me until I got 95% of my function back. And let me tell you- every inch of that 95% was earned through grit and grace.

But the body heals faster than the mind.

The mental toll? That part lingers. Grief doesn't have a clock, and trauma doesn't ask for permission to replay. I was grieving my parents, the loss of William, the shattering of my sense of safety and I was trying to hold it all together. The first therapist I had would literally fall asleep during our session. I knew then that that if I was going to heal, I had to advocate for myself. So, I searched and found a new therapist. She saw me. She helped me unpack all the dysfunction I'd been carrying from childhood and the toxic patterns I had normalized because my parents didn't know better. And she reminded me that I have the power to break those cycles.

One of the hardest lessons I had to learn was about friendship and family. After everything happened, so many people showed up, from washing my hair, sitting with me to helping me eat. But as time went on, those crowds faded. The calls stopped. The texts dried up. And I realized that part of my healing meant letting go of people I had outgrown. Some friendships didn't fit the new version of me. Some of my family didn't know how to show up for the woman I was becoming.

But God placed new people in my life. My cousin stepped in with love and consistency. My pastor and his daughter welcomed me into a chosen family where I felt seen, held, and safe. And even though I was still guarded, I let them in – because they gave me space to heal without judgement.

Healing taught me boundaries. It taught me to protect my peace. It taught me that not everyone deserves access to your most broken places. And it taught me that looking like you're okay and being okay are two very different things.

So if you see me and think I look fine, know this; I still cry. I still grieve. I still have days where I want to disappear. But I choose to show up. I choose to keep going.

Healing isn't a straight line, it's a winding road full of seatbacks and breakthroughs. And I'm still walking it.

But here's what I know for sure:
You can survive the unimaginable.
You can heal in your own time.
And you can build a life that feels like peace.

To every woman out there feeling trapped in trauma or buried in pain, let me say this:
You are not alone. There is hope. And there is life on the other side.

Keep going, sis.
Your healing is hold.
And you WILL survive.

Chapter 7

COURT AIN'T
closure

Nobody prepares you for what court feels like after surviving a nightmare. Not the therapists, not the victim witness coordinators, not the pamphlets they hand you. I walked into that courtroom four months after Satan tried to take my life. I was still recovering from surgery, still learning how to breathe without crying, still replaying May 2nd in my head like a horror movie.

And yet, there I was—standing ten feet from the man who tried to kill me.

They had us both step up to the podium. A computer screen separated us, but I could still see him — eyes locked on me, smiling. Not the smile of a man full of remorse, but the kind of smile that chills your bones. Cold. Detached. Excited even. Like seeing me in pain fed something dark inside him.

My fingertips were ice cold. I was shaking so bad I could barely breathe. I don't think people understand that trauma doesn't just live in your mind. It lives in your body. It lives in your nerves, in your breath, in the pit of your stomach. I was crying. Not because I was weak. But because I was facing the devil who had taken so much from me —and he didn't even blink.

That was just one of many days in court. Most were delayed. Some were canceled. One was even scheduled on my birthday. And each time I had to suit up in strength I didn't feel, just had to show up.

The scariest part? Having to look at all the evidence. They sat us down before the final court date and showed us the photos. My sweet friend William, deceased. Blood smeared across the walls of my house. My own handprint pressed against the wall where I tried to hit the panic button. It didn't look like a home anymore. It looked more like a murder scene. Because that's exactly what it was.

The security system had failed. He broke in through a second-story window, and the alarm never went off. I had to crawl — bloodied, naked, and barely alive —to my front door to get help. That's the part people don't understand. Survival is messy. It's bloody. It's humiliating. But it's still survival.

Satan continued to harass me even while incarcerated. On September 25, 2021, he emailed me from jail, claiming he missed me and still loved me. The next day, on September 26, 2021, he sent yet another email from jail, saying he couldn't stop thinking about me and missed the good times we shared.

He also contacted me on July 26 —the very day my mother died. That time, he used a "cousin" to send me a text message, attempting to cover his tracks by saying he didn't mean to dial my number and that he was suffering from memory loss. It was just another lie in a long pattern of manipulation.

In the end, I didn't even testify. He pled guilty before I had to take the stand. I think he thought he could manipulate the judge like he used to try to manipulate me. But the judge wasn't having it. He gave Satan life plus 66 years.

That's when the scene erupted.

Satan tried to stand up and perform for the courtroom —crying, apologizing, throwing words like, "sorry" around like they meant something. Then he flipped the table when he heard his sentence. He had to be dragged out by the bailiffs. His friends stormed out too — disrespectful, loud, and nasty while my sister have her testimony. No remorse. No decency.

But I noticed something. For all the noise his friends made, not one member of his family ever showed up in court. Not his mama. Not his sister. Just that one girl he cheated on me with, showing her face like she was somebody. That silence from his blood told me everything I needed to know about the man he really was.

When it was all over, I felt...relief, but also a deep ache. He threw his life away for nothing. Just evil, raw and unchecked. And I was left with scars —some visible, most not. I still cry sometimes thinking about the courtroom, the photos, the blood, the look on William's brother's face as he cried during sentencing. I had to step out. I couldn't take it.

But I showed up.

On July 18, 2023, he reached out again — this time by phone from prison. I was at work when the call came in. I didn't answer at first, but when the number called again, I picked up. The recording said, "You have a call from an inmate at (facility name)." I immediately reported the call. After an investigation, it was confirmed that he had once again deliberately attempted to contact me.

Following that incident, in July 2023, both the prison and victim witness services stepped in to block my phone and email from any future communication attempts. By August 2023, I made the decision to change my number. As must as it angered me to feel forced into that choice, I knew it was necessary for my peace and safety.

What I learned in court, showing up is powerful. Being a survivor in front of the one who tried to silence you is power. Having the system validate your pain is necessary —but it ain't closure. Closure is something you have to build, brick by brick.

On the following pages of this book, I've shared some of my favorite affirmations in hopes that it might help someone else the way that it has helped me.

acknowledgments

I am alive and thriving because of the love and support of so many amazing people. This list is in no way all-inclusive, but just a few of the people who saw me through some tough times and helped me live to tell the story.

First, I would like to thank William Simpson. I am alive today because of your sacrifice and your love.

I would like to thank my mom Sheila, my dad Cerdan and sister Angela for instilling greatness in me from the time I was born. I wouldn't be the person I am without you all. I Love you.

A big thank you to **Coach Debbie** for taking your time out to help me with this master plan and bringing it to life.

I would like to thank the medical staff at VCU Health for saving my life.

To my bestie, **Brittney**, thank you, thank you, thank you. Words can't express everything

I want to say. I just appreciate you showing up in every way possible in this process.

To my good friend **Dy'onna**, where do I start? You literally have been here every step of the way; you provided me with everything I needed those 5 days in the hospital and when I got out. Thank you, thank, thank you!

Jeff, thank you for taking me in. You took me in when you married my sister, but special shoutout to you for always making a way.

Chris and Natalia, thank you for doing all the things! From covering the broken windows to dealing with the contractor and helping me get moved, I appreciate you.

Jawon, Thank you and your family for being the angel on my shoulder as I move through this journey.

To my pastor, Thank you for being obedient to the messages God gave you. You could not have known every sermon you preached from

May 2021 through October was specifically to help me put my life back together.

Aunt Laverle, thank you for helping me get through my mom's passing during the time when I was still trying to heal from all that happened to me.

Damion, thank you for walking into my life at a time when I needed to heal and needed to have faith in humanity. Your gentle voice reminds me that it's going to be okay.

Erica, thank you for walking back into my house for the first time after my life was almost taken.

Jazmine, thank you for pouring your beautiful voice into my ear as I laid in the hospital bed holding on to dear life.

Sydney, thank you for continuing to provide me with love and a shoulder to cry on. Thank you for listening as I go through these traumatic emotions, and thank you for continuing to step up and take care of me in every way needed.

Christen, It's been a long time coming. Everything happens for a reason. God knew what he was doing when he reconnected us. I love you, girly.

Apryll, You've loved me like your own since the first day I stepped foot on the DOC. I love you.

Segal, You've seen it all, from the day the doctors took me out of the cast and sent me over to you for Arm and Hand therapy up until now. You've been here for me every step of the way, the smiles, laughs, and tears. I appreciate you for everything you do to help me regain use of my arm.

God, grant me the Serenity

To accept the things I cannot change... Courage to change the things I can, And Wisdom to know the difference.

Living one day at a time, Enjoying one moment at a time, Accepting hardship as the pathway to peace. Taking, as H s sinful world as it is, Not as would have it.

Trust that He will make all things right if I surrender to His will.

That I may be reasonably happy in this life,

And supremely happy with Him forever in the next. Amen.

———————————— SERENITY PRAYER

21-DAY
affirmation

 # Day 1

Even in my weakest moments, I still thank God that I'm alive. Even in my weakest moments, I thank God that the doctors are still taking care of me. Even in my weakest moments, I thank God all my needs are met, and I have more than enough.

_____

_____

_____

_____

_____

_____

_____

_____

Day 1

_____

_____

_____

_____

_____

_____

_____

_____

_____

_____

_____

_____

_____

_____

What do you do when you don't know what to do? You just keep trusting God.

_____

_____

_____

_____

_____

_____

_____

_____

_____

Day **2**

 # *Day 3*

"I'm grieving, but I'm going to get up and go to work. I'm going to dare to continue to show up in my life with my broken pieces and with my leftovers."

(Taken from Sarah Jakes Roberts).

_____

_____

_____

_____

_____

_____

_____

_____

Day 3

_____

_____

_____

_____

_____

_____

_____

_____

_____

_____

_____

_____

_____

_____

 # Day 4

Even in my weakest moments,
I'm still a warrior.

Day **4**

_____

_____

_____

_____

_____

_____

_____

_____

_____

_____

_____

_____

_____

I command my day to have PEACE!

_____

_____

_____

_____

_____

_____

_____

_____

_____

_____

Day **5**

_____

_____

_____

_____

_____

_____

_____

_____

_____

_____

_____

_____

_____

When it comes to abuse, you believe there's no way out. There's always help. There's always a way out.

(Taken from Rev. Donna Mulvey).

_____

_____

_____

_____

_____

_____

_____

_____

_____

Day **6**

_____

_____

_____

_____

_____

_____

_____

_____

_____

_____

_____

_____

_____

 # Day 7

Father, I have one assignment: to say what you want me to say. Fill me up, God. I turn my heart, my mouth, my soul over to you. Fill it until it touches every person in a domestic violence situation right now. Help them come out of the darkness.

_____

_____

_____

_____

_____

_____

_____

Day **7**

_____

_____

_____

_____

_____

_____

_____

_____

_____

_____

_____

_____

_____

 # *Day 8*

May the tears that I cry water the seeds I'm planting in my life right now.

Day 8

_____

_____

_____

_____

_____

_____

_____

_____

_____

_____

_____

_____

Thank you, God, for the friends I have by my side that wipe my tears when I cry.

_____

_____

_____

_____

_____

_____

_____

_____

_____

Day 9

_____

_____

_____

_____

_____

_____

_____

_____

_____

_____

_____

_____

_____

Day 10

Vengeance is mine. I will repay,
saith the Lord.

_____

_____

_____

_____

_____

_____

_____

_____

_____

_____

Day **10**

_____

_____

_____

_____

_____

_____

_____

_____

_____

_____

_____

_____

 # Day 11

Not by might, nor by power,
but your spirit God.

_____

_____

_____

_____

_____

_____

_____

_____

_____

_____

Day 11

_____

_____

_____

_____

_____

_____

_____

_____

_____

_____

_____

_____

_____

Day 12

*What's meant for you will always
have a way for you.*

_____

_____

_____

_____

_____

_____

_____

_____

_____

_____

Day **12**

_____

_____

_____

_____

_____

_____

_____

_____

_____

_____

_____

_____

Day 13

Take some time right now to celebrate yourself for all you have done. Do it for you.

_____

_____

_____

_____

_____

_____

_____

_____

_____

_____

Day **13**

_____

_____

_____

_____

_____

_____

_____

_____

_____

_____

_____

_____

_____

Day 14

Close those doors sis, peace is a priority.

_____

_____

_____

_____

_____

_____

_____

_____

_____

_____

_____

Day **14**

_____

_____

_____

_____

_____

_____

_____

_____

_____

_____

_____

_____

_____

 # Day 15

Stay in PEACE, not PIECES.

_____

_____

_____

_____

_____

_____

_____

_____

_____

_____

_____

Day **15**

_____

_____

_____

_____

_____

_____

_____

_____

_____

_____

_____

_____

_____

_____

Day 16

If God doesn't do anything else for me,
he's already done enough

_____

_____

_____

_____

_____

_____

_____

_____

_____

_____

Day **16**

_____

_____

_____

_____

_____

_____

_____

_____

_____

_____

_____

_____

_____

Day 17

Girl, it's going to be okay ... ACTUALLY,
it is already okay.

_____

_____

_____

_____

_____

_____

_____

_____

_____

_____

Day 17

_____

_____

_____

_____

_____

_____

_____

_____

_____

_____

_____

_____

_____

Day 18

There are going to be bad days,
but they are all still beautiful.

_____

_____

_____

_____

_____

_____

_____

_____

_____

_____

Day **18**

_____

_____

_____

_____

_____

_____

_____

_____

_____

_____

_____

_____

_____

 # Day 19

SET THAT STANDARD!

_____

_____

_____

_____

_____

_____

_____

_____

_____

_____

Day **19**

_____

_____

_____

_____

_____

_____

_____

_____

_____

_____

_____

_____

_____

Day 20

Self-love is the best love. Nobody can love you like you love yourself.

_____

_____

_____

_____

_____

_____

_____

_____

_____

_____

Day **20**

_____

_____

_____

_____

_____

_____

_____

_____

_____

_____

_____

_____

_____

Day 21

Lord, protect me from what I can't see.

_____

_____

_____

_____

_____

_____

_____

_____

_____

_____

_____

Day **21**
